Legends Poems

Compiled by John Foster

GW01465247

Contents

Acknowledgements

The Editor and Publisher wish to thank the following who have kindly given permission for the use of copyright material:

Andrew Collett for 'When I close my eyes' © 1996 Andrew Collett; Eric Finney for 'Thor' © 1996 Eric Finney; Tony Mitton for 'Anansi and the moon', 'The clever servant' and 'The fall of Icarus' all © 1996 Tony Mitton; Irene Rawnsley for 'The cat and the rat' © 1996 Irene Rawnsley.

When I close my eyes

When I close my eyes at night,
Lying in my bed,
My pillow fills with stories.
Legends fill my head.

Stories of mighty kings
And giants running tall,
Legends of fierce monsters
And fairies very small.

Stories from China,
Where dragons never die,
And legends from India
Where elephants can fly.

When I close my eyes at night,
Lying in my bed,
My pillow fills with stories.
Legends fill my head.

Andrew Collett

The fall of Icarus

Dedalus and Icarus
were prisoners long ago.
'But we'll escape,' said Dedalus.
'There's one way that I know.'

He took some wax and feathers,
then worked with skill and care.
He made two pairs of magic wings
to fly them through the air.

'Be careful, son,' said Dedalus.
'You must not fly too high,
or else the sun will melt your wings
and you'll fall from the sky.'

'And do not fly too near the waves.
The spray will weigh you down.
If you fall into the ocean,
You will be sure to drown.'

5

They strapped the wings upon their backs
and rose up in the air.
'The sun is hot,' said Dedalus.
'The sea is deep. Beware!'

6

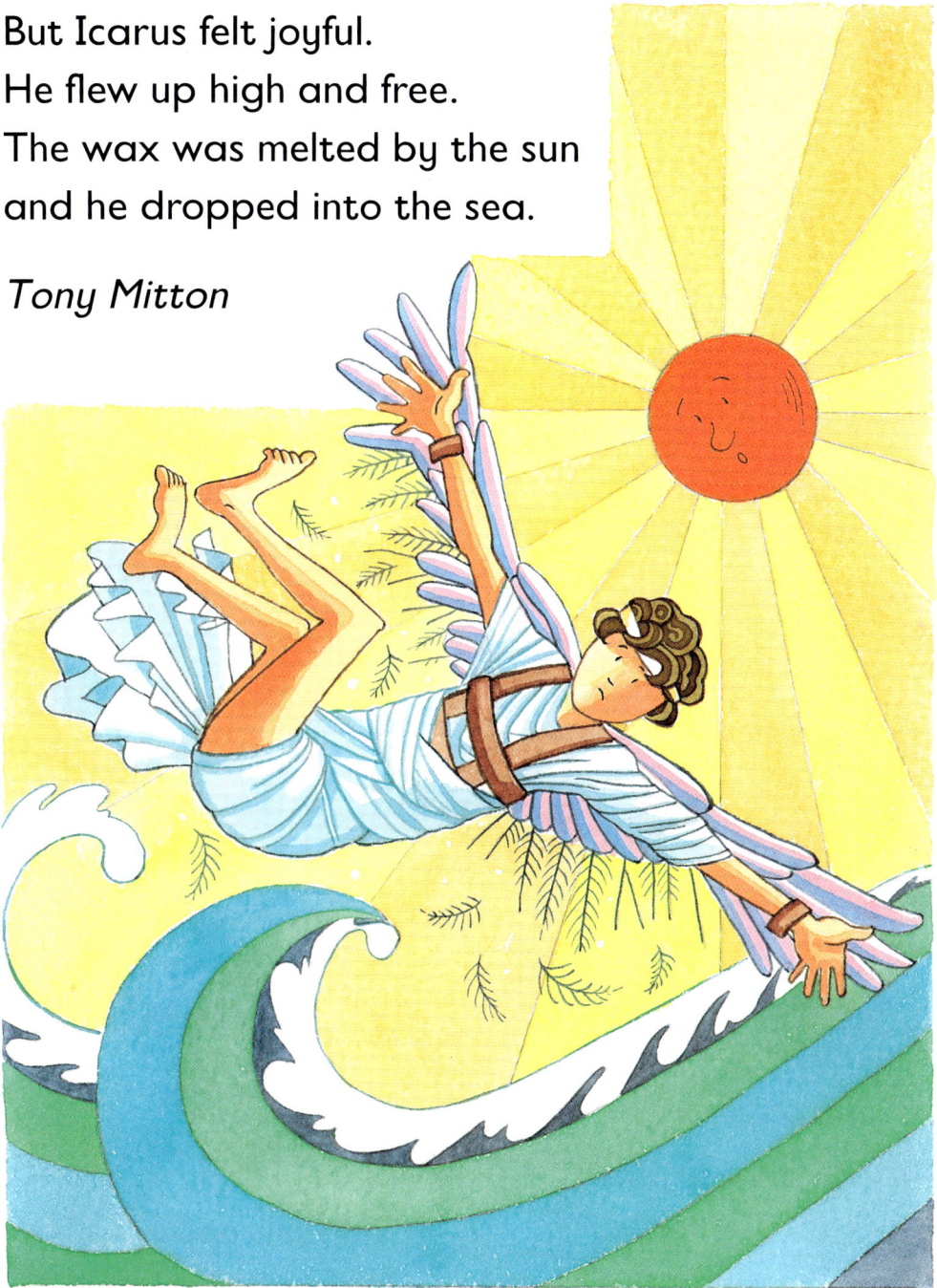

But Icarus felt joyful.
He flew up high and free.
The wax was melted by the sun
and he dropped into the sea.

Tony Mitton

The clever servant

A merchant called his servants,
one, two, three.
'Who can fill this room
for one rupee?'

The first met a farmer
and bought a pile of straw.
He took it to the merchant
and spread it on the floor.

The second bought some earth
from an old ditch-digger.
'Better!' said the merchant.
'This pile is bigger.'

But the third bought a candle
and lit it that night.
'The winner!' said the merchant.
'The room is full of light!'

Tony Mitton

The cat and the rat

A cat and a rat
once went to sea
in a boat they made
from the trunk of a tree.

But the sun was hot
and the sea was deep.
The rat grew hungry.
The cat fell asleep.

Rat nibbled a meal
from the side of the boat.
It tasted good.
They were still afloat,

So he nibbled and nibbled
a little bit more.
Soon the boat was sinking.
Rat swam to the shore.

The wet cat in a fury
followed him fast.
Rat hid in a hole
till the danger was past.

And since that time
where the story ends,
cats and rats
have never been friends.

Irene Rawnsley

Anansi and the moon

Spiderman Anansi
went walking in the night.
Suddenly he noticed
a shining silver light.

He went to have a closer look,
and what was it he found?
A great big shiny silver pearl
lying on the ground.

'Ah!', cried Anansi.
'What a lovely sight!
I'll take it home to give my boys,
and fill them with delight.'

But when Anansi showed it,
the boys could not agree.
They all began to argue, saying,
'Give it just to me!'

So, in the end, Anansi
threw it far and high.
It settled there among the stars,
floating in the sky.

And if you look at night-time
you'll see it hanging there:
a lovely round and silver moon
for all of us to share.

Tony Mitton

Thor

Tonight, Thor, god of thunder
Is riding through the sky:
Listen as his wagon
Rumbles by.

When he flings his mighty hammer,
Watch the sky turn black.
See the lightning flashing.
Hear the thunder crack.

Eric Finney

Printed in Hong Kong